REMARKABLE JUMBO JETS

BY NATALIE HUMPHREY

Gareth Stevens
PUBLISHING

Please visit our website, www.garethstevens.com. For a free color catalog of all our high-quality books, call toll free 1-800-542-2595 or fax 1-877-542-2596.

Portions of this work were originally authored by Kenny Allen and published as *Jumbo Jets*. All new material in this edition is authored by Natalie Humphrey.

Cataloging-in-Publication Data

Names: Humphrey, Natalie.
Title: Remarkable jumbo jets / Natalie Humphrey.
Description: New York : Gareth Stevens Publishing, 2023. | Series: Mega machines! | Includes glossary and index.
Identifiers: ISBN 9781538283158 (pbk.) | ISBN 9781538283172 (library bound) | ISBN 9781538283189 (ebook)
Subjects: LCSH: Jet planes–Juvenile literature. | Jet transports–Juvenile literature.
Classification: LCC TL547.H86 2023 | DDC 629.133'349–dc23

Published in 2023 by
Gareth Stevens Publishing
2455 Clinton Street
Buffalo, NY 14224

Designer: Deanna Paternostro
Editor: Natalie Humphrey

Photo credits: Cover, p. 1 Skycolors/Shutterstock.com; pp. 3, 4, 6, 8, 10, 12, 14, 16, 18, 20, 21 (bottom), 22, 23, 24 Nataliia K/Shutterstock.com; p. 5, 21 (top) G Tipene/Shutterstock.com; p. 7 Dimitrios Karamitros/Shutterstock.com; p. 9 Dolfilms/Shutterstock.com; p. 11 schusterbauer.com/Shutterstock.com; p. 13 supakitswn/Shutterstock.com; p. 15 Stoyan Yotov/Shutterstock.com; p. 17 Danc47667/Shutterstock.com; p. 19 vaalaa/Shutterstock.com.

Printed in the United States of America

Some of the images in this book illustrate individuals who are models. The depictions do not imply actual situations or events.

CPSIA compliance information: Batch #CW23GS: For further information contact Gareth Stevens at 1-800-542-2595.

Find us on

CONTENTS

Boldface words appear in the glossary.

Giant Planes

Jumbo jets are some of the biggest planes out there! Many of these huge planes can carry hundreds of passengers. They can travel more than 7,700 **nautical miles** (14,300 km) in one trip. But the size of this mega machine isn't the only amazing thing about it!

Prepare For Liftoff!

How does a plane stay in the air? It's because of a force called **lift**! During takeoff, the plane uses **thrust** from its engines to go fast. Air moving over the plane's wing moves faster than air moving under it. This causes lift, which pushes the plane into the air.

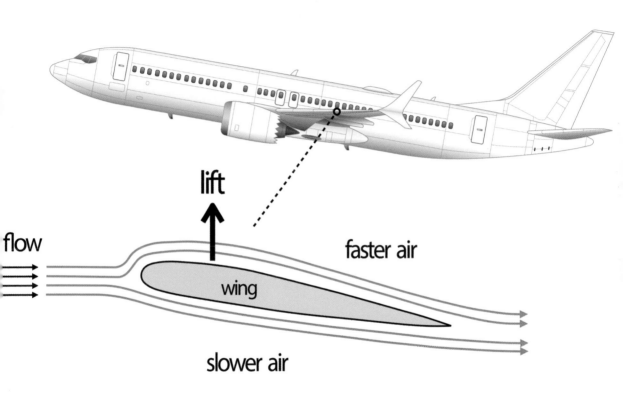

lift

flow

faster air

wing

slower air

The Pilot's Seat

At the front of a plane is a space called a cockpit. The cockpit is where the **pilot** and copilot sit and fly the plane. The cockpit has many controls and screens. The pilot uses these to watch the weather and fly the plane.

Wide-Bodied

Another name for a jumbo jet is a wide-body plane. Wide-body planes have two **aisles** between three groups of seats. Regular passenger planes have one aisle between seats. The widest jumbo jets have enough seats for up to 10 people in one row!

AISLES

Two Stories

Another way jumbo jets have fit more people is by having two separate floors. These two-story planes have carried more than 800 passengers! Some **private** jumbo jets have enough space for a bedroom, bathrooms, and even a kitchen!

Jet Engines

Engines power jumbo jets. They have two, three, or four engines! Jumbo jet engines need to be big and powerful to keep the plane in the air. Some jumbo jet engines are bigger than elephants!

Space for Cargo

Because jumbo jets are so large, they have a lot of space for **cargo**. The Airbus Beluga XL is named after a whale. It was made extra large to carry very large cargo. This jumbo jet can carry cargo over 154 feet (47 m) long!

Airbus A380

One of the biggest jumbo jets is the Airbus A380. Sometimes called a superjumbo jet, the A380 can carry 850 passengers. The A380 is so large, it can't land at every airport! Some airports had to change their runways just so the A380 could fit.

The Future of Jumbo Jets

Jumbo jets are amazing mega machines, but bigger isn't always better. Because jumbo jets are so big, they cost a lot to make. Jumbo jets also burn a lot of fuel and create **pollution**. Today, jumbo jets are being flown less often.

Mega Machine Facts: Airbus A380

Length: 239 feet (73 m)

Speed: 634 miles (1,020 km) per hour

Number of Passenger Seats: up to 853

Cost: up to $445 million

GLOSSARY

aisle: A path for walking between seats

cargo: Goods carried by a plane, train, or truck.

lift: The force that pushes planes and other objects into the air.

nautical mile: The unit used by ships and planes to measure distance.

pilot: Someone who flies a plane

private: Owned by only one person.

pollution: Matter in the water or air, or on lane that harms living things.

thrust: The force that pushes an object forward.

FOR MORE INFORMATION

BOOKS

Gall, Chris. *Jumbo: The Making of the Boeing 747*. New York, NY: Roaring Brook Press, 2020.

Rogers, Marie. *Giant Jumbo Jets*. New York, NY: PowerKids Press, 2022.

WEBSITES

Airbus Discovery Space
www.airbus.com/en/sustainability/airbus-foundation/ youth-development/discovery-space
Learn more about the history of flight and what some airplane makers are planning for the future!

DK Findout!: Jumbo Jets
www.dkfindout.com/us/transportation/history-aircraft/jumbo-jet/
Learn more about jumbo jets history and how they work.

INDEX